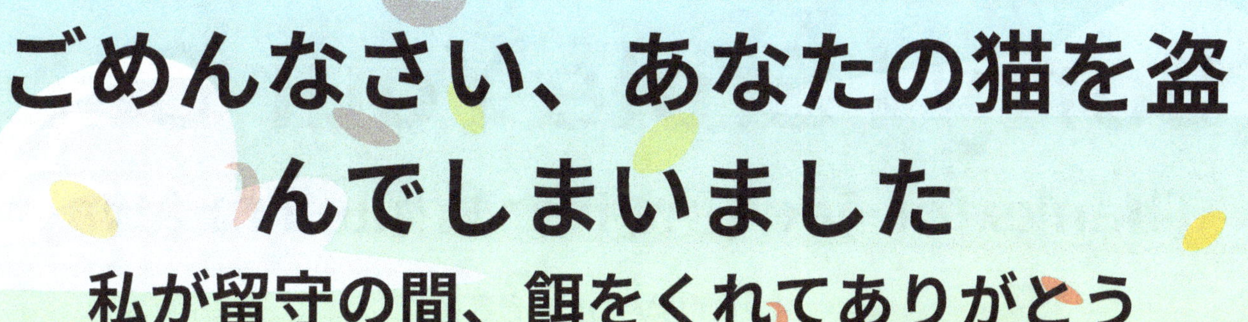

ごめんなさい、あなたの猫を盗んでしまいました

私が留守の間、餌をくれてありがとう

Marcy Schaaf

Japanese

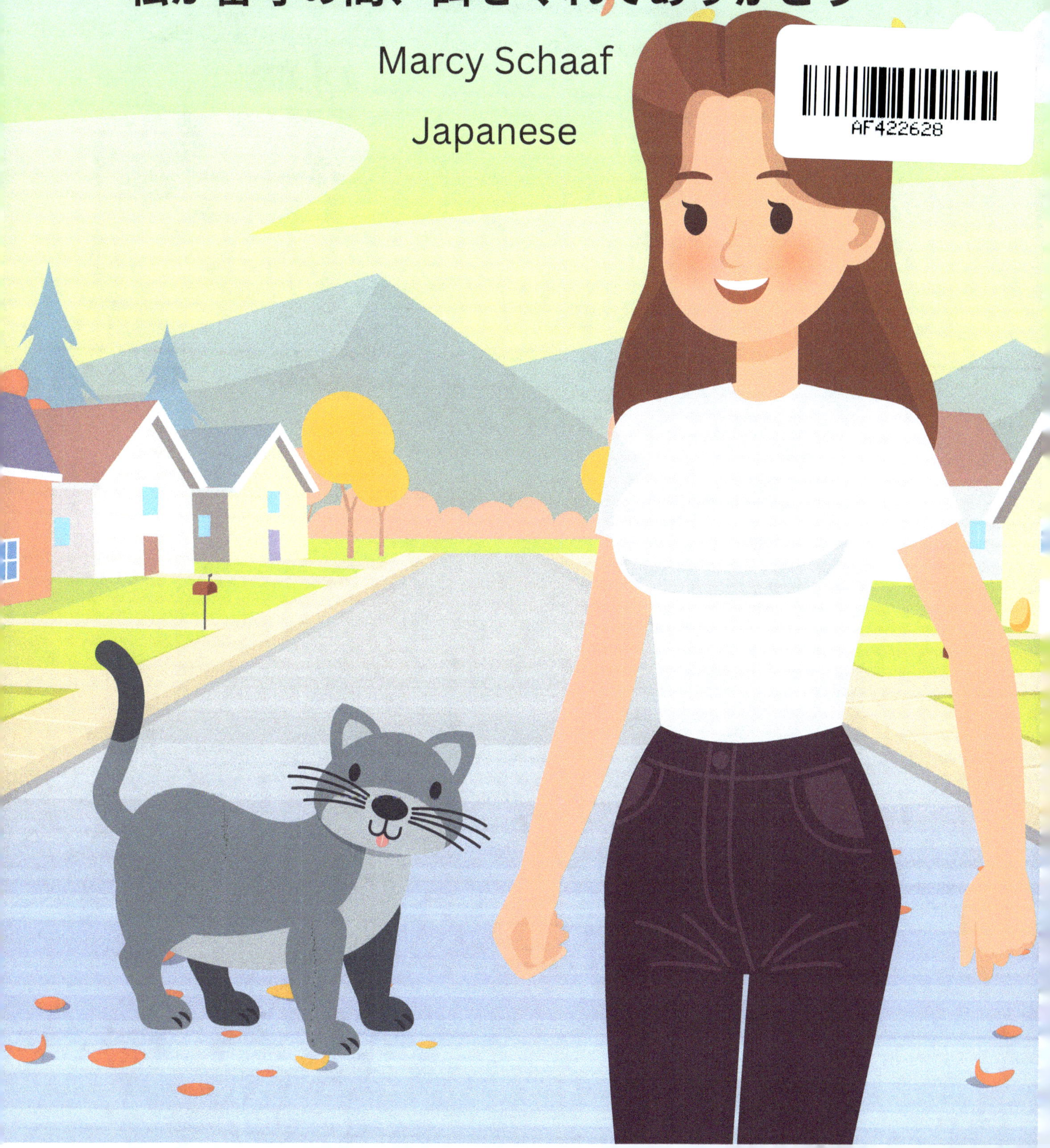

Sorry I Stole Your Cat

Thanks for Feeding Her While I'm Away

Marcy Schaaf

Meet Delila, the lovable cat whose life takes an unexpected turn when her family gets a new puppy. Feeling left out and overwhelmed, Delila finds a new home next door with a kind single lady. But when the lady goes on vacation, Delila's old family steps in to help, and everyone learns a valuable lesson about change and love.

Sorry I Stole Your Cat, Thanks for Feeding Her While I'm Away is a true story from Pahoa, Hawaii.

This delightful tale shows that even when life changes, it can still be filled with love, happiness, and new beginnings.
Join Delila on her heartwarming adventure and discover that no matter what happens, it's okay to embrace change!

This book is dedicated to Lux and Tula, the amazing kids next door.

Thank you for sharing your wonderful cat, Delila, with such open hearts and allowing her love to fill my life. Your kindness and understanding meant the world to both of us. Delila brought joy and comfort to my home when I needed it the most, and I hope she brought just as much happiness to yours.

Life has a funny way of bringing us together in the most unexpected ways, and I'm so grateful that our paths crossed. Lux and Tula, your generosity and love made all the difference, and for that, I am forever thankful.

Your friend and Neighbor,
Marcy Schaaf

Copywrite2024 @Marcy Schaaf Sorry I stole Your Cat
Thanks for Feeding Her While I'm Alway

Once there was a cat named
Delila.

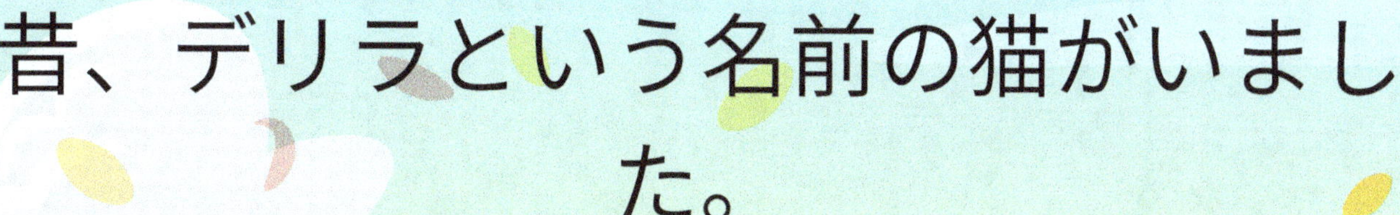

昔、デリラという名前の猫がいました。

She lived with a family of four.

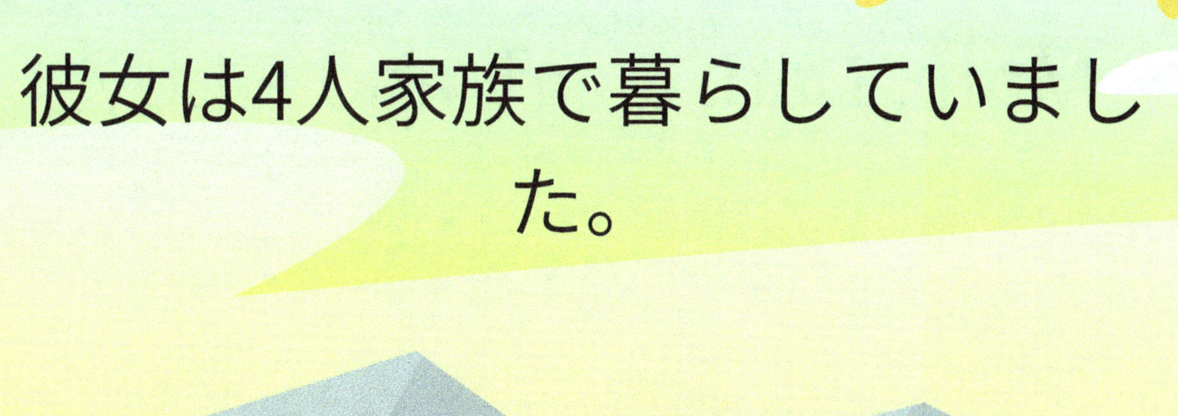

彼女は4人家族で暮らしていました。

Mom, Dad, a girl, and a boy.

お母さん、お父さん、女の子、そして男の子。

One day
they got a new puppy.

ある日、彼らは新しい子犬を飼いました。

The puppy ate Delila's food.

子犬はデリラの食べ物を食べました。

The puppy chased her around.

子犬は彼女を追いかけ回した。

It even took her spot in bed!

ベッドで彼女の場所まで占領してしまいました！

Delila was old and
didn't wanna play with the puppy.

デリラは年老いていて、子犬と遊び
たくなかった。

She found a peaceful
home next door.

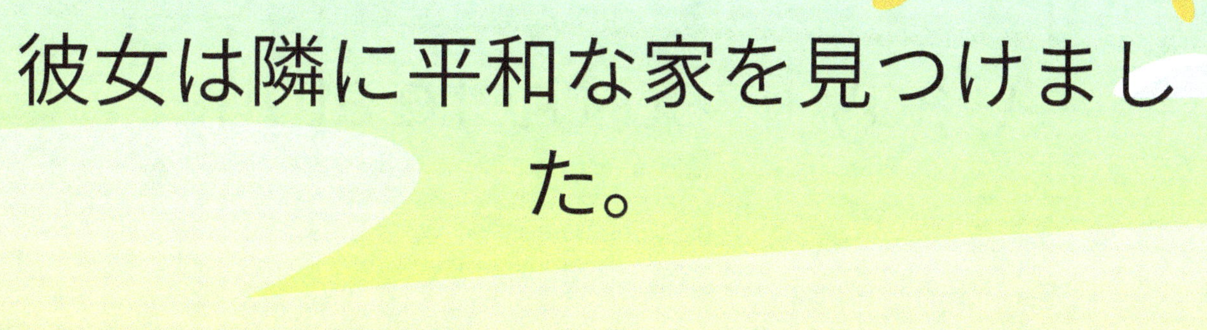

彼女は隣に平和な家を見つけました。

A lady lived there alone.

そこには一人の女性が一人で住んで
いました。

The lady planted catnip for Delila.

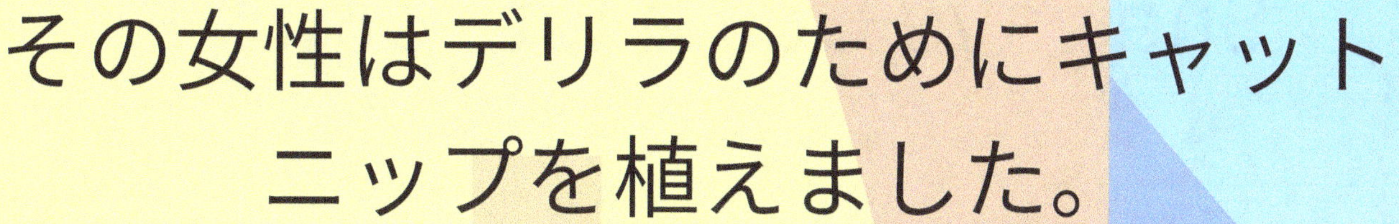

その女性はデリラのためにキャット
ニップを植えました。

She gave Delila lots of love.

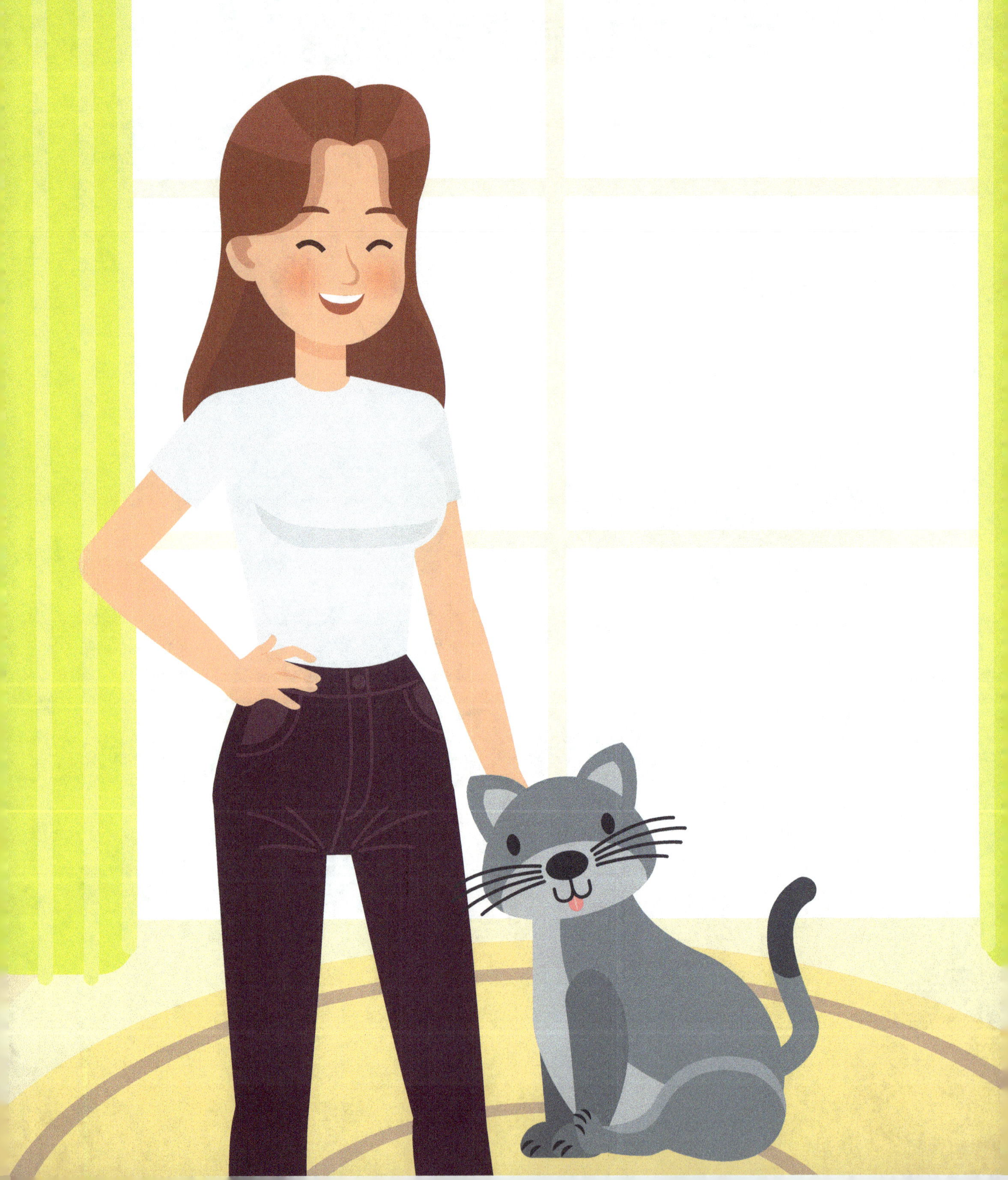

彼女はデリラにたくさんの愛を与えました。

Delila had a new comfy spot.

In the lady's master bedroom.

デリラは新しい快適な場所を見つけ
ました。

女性の主寝室にて。

One day the lady
went on vacation.

ある日、その女性は休暇に出かけました。
TAXI
TRAVELER

She asked the kids
next door for help.

彼女は隣の子供たちに助けを求めた。

"Sorry I stole your cat," she said.

「あなたの猫を盗んでごめんなさい」と彼女は言った。

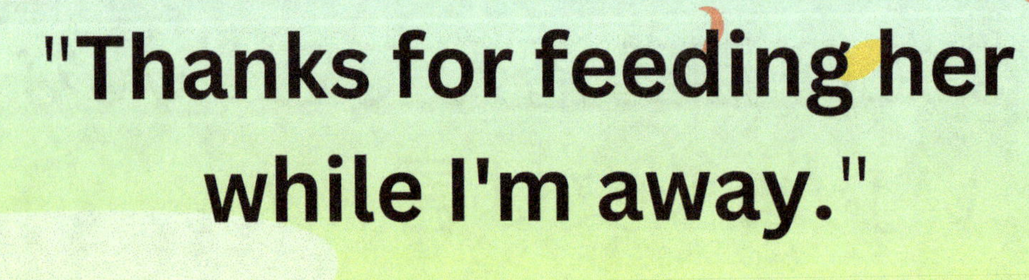

"Thanks for feeding her while I'm away."

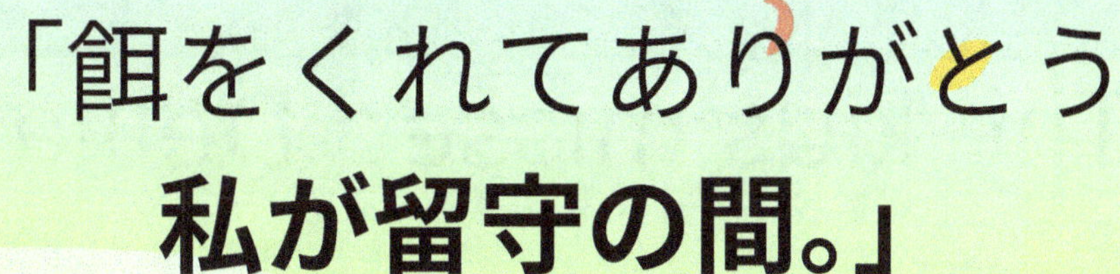

「餌をくれてありがとう
私が留守の間。」

The kids missed Delila.

子供たちはデリラがいなくて寂しかった。

They were happy to help.

彼らは喜んで手伝ってくれました。

They fed Delila every day.

彼らはデリラに毎日餌を与えた。

They played with her, too.

彼らも彼女と遊びました。

Delila felt loved and happy.

デリラは愛され、幸せを感じました。

She had the best of both worlds.

彼女は両方の世界の良いところを持っていました。

A quiet home and playful kids.

静かな家庭と遊び好きな子供たち。

When the lady returned,
she thanked them.

女性は戻ってきて彼らに感謝した。

Delila purred contentedly.

She was right where
she should be!

デリラは満足そうに喉を鳴らした。

彼女はまさにいるべき場所にいたの
です！

Life changes sometimes
and that's okay.

人生は時々変わる
それは大丈夫です。

The End.

The real kids next door

Books By Schaaf

www.BookBySchaaf.com

Find us at: